Introduction

Our staff has seen many wonderful afghans through the years, but this collection is more exciting to us than most—because they are ***Definitely Different Afghans***. Designer Diana Lynn Sippel has an innovative approach and has spotlighted an unusual and very interesting technique in each of these five afghans.

Double Take, shown on the front cover and page 12, features squares with double-thick centers—a super energy saving idea for winter.

Woven Marvel, shown on the back cover, is crocheted and woven. Making this afghan is as much fun as weaving potholders-you'll feel like a kid again.

Winding Rosebuds and *Spiral Skyway*, shown on pages 10 and 11, are perfect for ripple lovers. The centers of the strips are simple zig-zags (like a ripple) that twist together for a distinctive new look.

Floral Magic, page 9, has a kaleidoscope feel to it, with colorful hexagons and elongated single crochets that magically create pretty flower centers.

If you would like to learn more about our designer, please check out Diana's website at: www.dianalynnsdesigns.com

It's no surprise that a forward thinking designer like Diana would also have a website.

Abbreviations and Symbols

beg .... begin(ning)
BL(s) .... back loop(s)
BPdc ... back post double crochet(s)
ch(s) .... chain(s)
CL(s) .... cluster(s)
dc .... double crochet(s)
dec .... decrease(-ing)
dtrc .... double triple crochet(s)
FL(s) .... front loop(s)
FPdc ... front post double crochet(s)
hdc .... half double crochet(s)
lp(s) ....loop(s)
patt .... pattern
prev .... previous
rem .... remain(ing)
rep .... repeat(ing)
rnd(s) .... round(s)
sc .... single crochet(s)
sk .... skip
sl .... slip
sl st(s) .... slip stitch(es)
sp(s) .... space(s)
st(s) .... stitch(es)
tog ....together
trc .... triple crochet(s)
YO .... yarn over

* An asterisk (or double asterisks **) is used to mark the beginning of a portion of instructions to be worked more than once; thus, "rep from * twice more" means after working the instructions once, repeat the instructions following the asterisk twice more (3 times in all).

† The dagger (or double daggers ††) identifies a portion of instructions that will be repeated again later in the same row or round.

— The number after a long dash at the end of a row or round indicates the number of stitches you should have when the row or round has been completed. The long dash can also be used to indicate a completed stitch such as a decrease, a shell, or a cluster.

() Parentheses are used to enclose instructions which should be worked the exact number of times specified immediately following the parentheses, such as "(2 sc in next dc, sc in next dc) twice." They are also used to set off and clarify a group of stitches that are to be worked all into the same space or stitch, such as "(2 dc, ch 1, 2 dc) in corner sp."

[] Brackets and () parentheses are used to provide additional information to clarify instructions.

Join - join with a sl st unless otherwise specified.

The patterns in this book are written using United States terminology. Terms which have different English equivalents are noted below.

United States	English
single crochet (sc)	double crochet (dc)
half double crochet (hdc)	half treble (htr)
double crochet (dc)	treble (tr)
triple crochet (trc)	double treble (dtr)
double triple crochet (dtrc)	triple treble (trtr)
skip (sk)	miss
slip stitch (sl st)	slip stitch (ss) or "single crochet"
gauge	tension
yarn over (YO)	yarn over hook (YOH)
worsted weight	4-ply

A Word about the Yarns

These wonderful afghans have been created using the following yarns: Caron Wintuk®; Coats and Clark Red Heart® TLC®; and Spinrite® Berella® "4"® and Berella® So Soft®. Any yarns that achieve the specified gauges may be substitued.

A Word about Gauge

A correct stitch gauge is very important. Please take the time to work a stitch gauge swatch about 4" x 4". Measure the swatch. If the number of stitches and rows are fewer than indicated under "Gauge" in the pattern, your hook is too large. Try another swatch with a smaller size hook. If the number of stitches and rows are more than indicated under "Gauge" in the pattern, your hook is too small. Try another swatch with a larger size hook.

Stitch Guide

Chain - ch:
YO, draw through lp on hook.

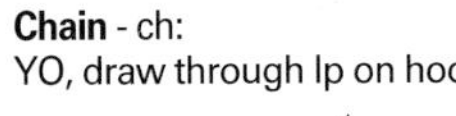

Single Crochet - sc:
Insert hook in st, YO and draw through, YO and draw through both lps on hook.

Half Double Crochet - hdc:
YO, insert hook in st, YO, draw through, YO and draw through all 3 lps on hook.

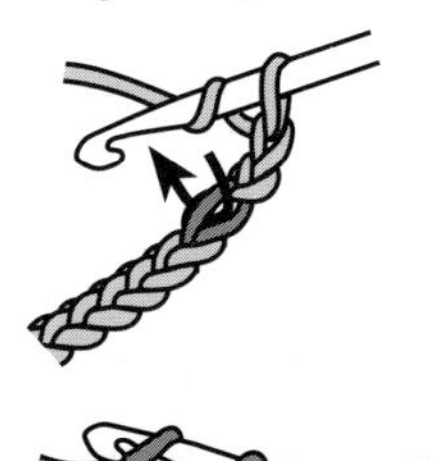

Double Crochet - dc:
YO, insert hook in st, YO, draw through, (YO and draw through 2 lps on hook) twice.

Triple Crochet - trc:
YO twice, insert hook in st, YO, draw through, (YO and draw through 2 lps on hook) 3 times.

Slip Stitch - sl st:
(a) Used for Joinings
Insert hook in indicated st, YO and draw through st and lp on hook.

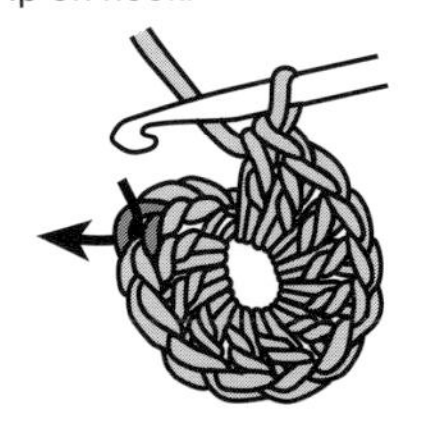

(b) Used for Moving Yarn Over
Insert hook in st, YO draw through st and lp on hook.

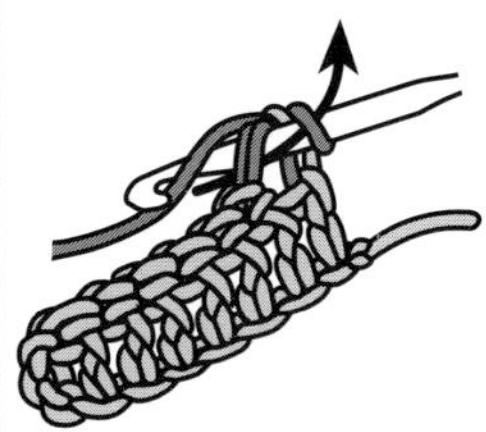

Front Loop - FL:
The front loop is the loop toward you at the top of the stitch.

Back Loop - BL:
The back loop is the loop away from you at the top of the stitch.

Post:
The post is the vertical part of the stitch.

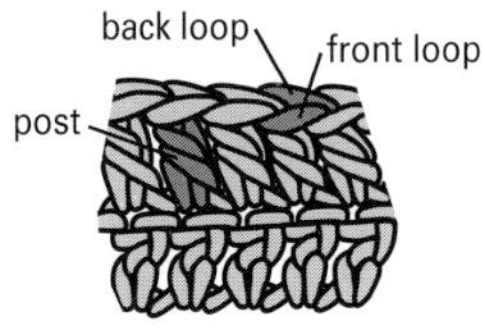

Overcast Stitch is worked loosely to join crochet pieces.

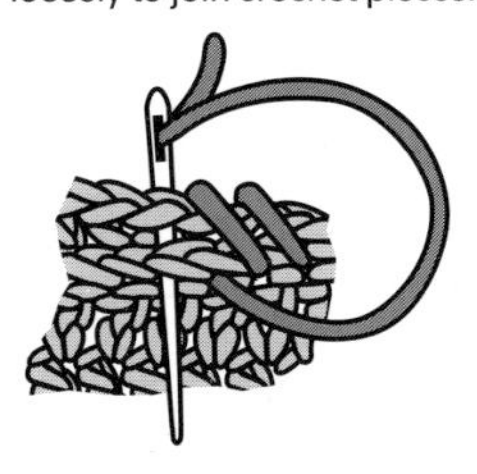

Spiral Skyway

Size:
About 42" x 58"

Materials:
Worsted weight yarn, 36 oz (2520 yds, 1080 g)
    lt blue; 7 oz (490 yds, 210 g) med blue; 4 oz
    (280 yds, 120 g) white
Size I (5.5mm) crochet hook, or size required
    for gauge
Note: Photographed model made with Spinrite®
Berella® So Soft® Pale Blue #9851; Medium Blue
#9856; and White #9848.

Gauge:
4 dc = 1"
4 dc rows = 3"

Pattern Stitches

Long Double Crochet (long dc):
YO, insert hook in sp indicated, draw up lp to
height of working rnd, (YO, draw through 2 lps on
hook) twice—long dc made.

Cluster (CL):
YO, insert hook in lp indicated on 2nd rnd below,
YO, draw through 2 lps on hook; sk next long dc,
YO, insert hook in next lp indicated on 2nd rnd
below, YO, draw through 2 lps on hook; with
color indicated, YO and draw through all 3 lps on
hook—CL made.

Long Single Crochet (long sc):
Insert hook in st indicated on 2nd rnd below,
draw up lp to height of working rnd, YO and draw
through 2 lps on hook—long sc made.

Instructions

Panel (make 9)

Center Braid
With lt blue, ch 635, mark 316th ch from beg.

In 5th ch from hook work (dc, ch 1) 3 times (beg 4
skipped chs count as a dc and a ch-1 sp); dc in same
ch—beg 5-dc group made; dc in next 2 chs; keeping
last lp of each dc on hook, (sk next ch, dc in next ch)
5 times; YO and draw through all 6 lps on hook—
cluster made; dc in next 2 chs; † in next ch work (dc,
ch 1) 4 times; dc in same ch—5-dc group made; dc

in next 2 chs; keeping last lp of each dc on hook, (sk
next ch, dc in next ch) 5 times; YO and draw through
all 6 lps on hook—cluster made; dc in next 2 chs †;
rep from † to † 19 times more; in marked ch work
(dc, ch 1) 9 times; dc in same ch—10-dc group
made; dc in next 2 chs; keeping last lp of each dc on
hook, (sk next ch, dc in next ch) 5 times; YO and
draw through all 6 lps on hook—cluster made; dc in
next 2 chs; rep from † to † 20 times; in next ch work
(dc, ch 1) 5 times—ending 5-dc group made; draw
up long lp on hook, remove hook, do not cut yarn.

Hold center braid with 10-dc group at top; weave
sides over and under each other (see photo); at
opposite end, re-insert hook in long lp and join in
3rd ch of beg 4 skipped chs, forming a second 10-dc
group. Weave beg yarn end through base of ending
5-dc group to hold 10-dc group together.

continued

Spiral Skyway

Center Border:
Rnd 1:
Ch 1, sc in same ch as joining; (ch 3, sc in next dc) twice; working along next side, † ch 4, sc in unused lp at base of 3rd dc of next cluster, ch 4, sc in 3rd dc of next 5-dc group †; rep from † to † 19 times more; ch 4, sc in unused lp at base of 3rd dc of next cluster, ch 4, sc in 3rd dc of next 10-dc group; ch 3, (sc in next dc, ch 3) 4 times; sc in next dc; rep from † to † 20 times; ch 4, sc in unused lp at base of 3rd dc of next cluster, ch 4, sc in 3rd dc of next 5-dc group; ch 3, (sc in next dc, ch 3) twice; join in first sc.

Rnd 2:
Ch 1, sc in same sc; (4 sc in next ch-3 sp, sc in next sc) twice; (4 sc in next ch-4 sp, sc in next sc) 42 times; (4 sc in next ch-3 sp, sc in next sc) 5 times; (4 sc in next ch-4 sp, sc in next sc) 42 times; (4 sc in next ch-3 sp, sc in next sc) twice; 4 sc in next ch-3 sp; join in first sc. Finish off.

Rnd 3:
With med blue, make lp on hook and join with an sc in BL of first sc to left of joining; working in BLs only, sc in next 3 sc, working over next sc, long dc (see Pattern Stitches on page 5) in same sp on center as next sc on 2nd rnd below; * working in BLs only, sc in next 4 sc, working over next sc, long dc in same sp on center as next sc on 2nd rnd below; rep from * around; join in first sc. Finish off.

Note: When changing colors, work last st until 2 lps of st remain on hook, draw new color through. Carry color not in use, working over carried strand until needed.

Rnd 4:
With lt blue, make lp on hook and join with an sc in BL of 2nd sc to right of next long dc; working in BLs only of sc on working rnd and in unused lps on 2nd rnd below, sc in next sc changing to white; * CL (see Pattern Stitches on page 5) over lp on 2nd rnd below sc just worked and in lp on 2nd rnd below sc after long dc, drawing lt blue through all 3 lps on hook; on working rnd, sk long dc, sc in next 4 sc, changing to white in last sc; rep from * to last long dc; working in unused lps on 2nd rnd below, CL over lp on 2nd rnd below sc just worked and in lp on 2nd rnd below sc after long dc, drawing lt blue through all 3 lps on hook; on working rnd, sk long dc, sc in next 2 sc; join in joining sc. Cut white.

Rnd 5:
Ch 1, sc in same sc and in next sc; * working over next CL, long sc (see Pattern Stitches on page 5) in next long dc on 2nd rnd below; on working rnd, sk next CL, sc in next 4 sc; rep from * to last CL; working over next CL, long sc in next long dc on 2nd rnd below; on working rnd, sk next CL, sc in next 2 sc; join in first sc.

Finish off and weave in all ends.

Assembly
Hold two panels with right sides together and carefully match corresponding CLs. Sew together using overcast stitch (see Stitch Guide on page 4) through BLs only of corresponding sts, beginning and ending with 3rd CL from end of each 10-dc group.

Repeat with remaining panels.

Floral Magic

Size:
About 42" x 55"

Materials:
Worsted weight yarn, 3 oz (210 yds, 90 g) each of 9 assorted colors; 17 oz (1190 yds, 510 g) each off white and green

Size I (5.5mm) crochet hook, or size required for gauge

Size 16 tapestry needle

Note: Our photographed model made with Spinrite® Berella® "4"® Natural #8940; Pale Glacier Green #8729; Bold Orchid #8730; Pale Tapestry Gold #8887; Light Tapestry Gold #8886; Orchid #8731; Rose #8921; Arbutus #8922; Pale Teal #8846; China Rose #8923; and Light Antique Rose #8815.

Gauge:
hexagon = 4" x 4" (from point to point)

Pattern Stitch

Long Single Crochet (long sc):
With yarn behind work, insert hook in st indicated and draw up lp to height of working rnd; YO and draw through 2 lps on hook—long sc made.

Instructions

Hexagon (make 182)
With any of assorted colors, ch 5; join to form a ring.

Rnd 1 (right side):
Ch 1, 12 sc in ring; join in first sc—12 sc.

Rnd 2:
Ch 1, 3 sc in same sc; sc in next sc; * 3 sc in next sc; sc in next sc; rep from * 4 times more; join in first sc—24 sc.

Rnd 3:
Ch 1, sc in same sc; 3 sc in next sc; * sc in next 3 sc, 3 sc in next sc; rep from * 4 times more; sc in next 2 sc; join in first sc—36 sc.

Rnd 4:
Ch 1, sc in same sc and in next 2 sc (mark last sc worked); * sc in next 6 sc; rep from * 4 times more; sc in next 3 sc; join in first sc. Finish off.

Rnd 5:
With off white make lp on hook and join with an sc in marked sc; 2 sc in same sc; *† long sc (see Pattern Stitch) in next sc on 2nd rnd below, long sc in next sc on 3rd rnd below, long sc in next sc on 4th rnd below, long sc in next sc on 3rd rnd below, long sc in next sc on 2nd rnd below †; 3 sc in next sc; rep from * 4 times more, then rep from † to † once; join in joining sc. Finish off.

Rnd 6:
With green make lp on hook and join with an sc in any st; sc in each rem st; join in joining sc.

Finish off and weave in all ends.

continued

Assembly

Referring to Diagram A for placement, join hexagons tog. To join, hold two hexagons with right sides together; working through BLs only with green and overcast st (see Stitch Guide on page 4) sew tog along one side beginning and ending with corner sc. Repeat until a strip of 14 hexagons have been joined. Repeat joining a strip of 13 hexagons. Sew the strips together alternating strips of 14 hexagons and 13 hexagons, beginning and ending with strips of 14 hexagons.

Border

Hold afghan with right side facing you and one short edge at top; with green make lp on hook and join with an sc in BL of corner sc indicated on Diagram A, 2 sc in same sc; † working along side of same hexagon, sc in BLs of next 7 sc, sc in next seam; working across edge of next hexagon, sc in BLs of next 7 sc, sc in next seam; working along side of next hexagon, sc in BLs of next 7 sc, 3 sc in next sc—corner made; working across edge of same hexagon, sc in BLs of next 7 sc, 3 sc in next sc—corner made †; rep from † to † 5 times more; working along next side of same hexagon, sc in BLs of next 7 sc, 3 sc in next sc—corner made; working along next side of same hexagon, sc in BLs of next 7 sc, sc in next seam; †† working along side of next hexagon, sc in BLs of next 7 sc, 3 sc in next sc—corner made; working along next side of same hexagon, sc in BLs of next 7 sc, sc in next seam ††; rep from †† to †† 11 times more; working around next hexagon, * sc in BLs of next 7 sc, 3 sc in next sc—corner made; rep from * twice more; rep from † to † 6 times; working along next side of same hexagon, sc in BLs of next 7 sc, 3 sc in next sc—corner made; working along next side of same hexagon, sc in BLs of next 7 sc, sc in next seam; rep from †† to †† 12 times; working around next hexagon, ** sc in BLs of next 7 sc, 3 sc in next sc—corner made; rep from ** once more; sc in BLs of next 7 sc; join in joining sc.

Finish off and weave in all ends.

Diagram A

Start border here ⟶

Flowers magically appear as you work white elongated single crochet stitches into the center of each colorful hexagon. Your crochet hook becomes a magic wand!

Winding Rosebuds

Begin each strip with white rippling vines and then add a border of dainty rosebuds and leaves. This afghan is as beautiful as an arbor of miniature roses!

Each center strip begins with rippling double crochet stitches which easily twist together. Add the creative border, join the strips, sit back and dream of blue skies on a sunny day.

Double Take

Believe it or not, each double thick center is crocheted in the round with no increasing, and then flattened to form a square. Notice how the borders come together and form stars.

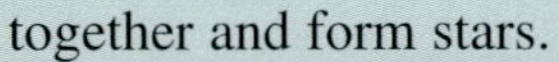

Double Take

Size:
About 48" x 63"

Materials:
Worsted weight yarn, 50 oz (3500 yds, 1500 g) variegated; 25 oz (1750 yds, 750 g) each off white and coral

Size H (5mm) crochet hook, or size required for gauge

Note: Photographed model made with Coats and Clark Red Heart® TLC® Country Club #5978; Natural #5017; and Coral Rose #5730.

Gauge:
7 sc = 2"
4 sc rows = 1"
center of square = 4$\frac{1}{2}$" x 4$\frac{1}{2}$"
completed square = 7$\frac{1}{2}$" x 7$\frac{1}{2}$"

Pattern Stitch

Long Double Crochet (long dc):
YO, insert hook in st or sp indicated, draw up lp to height of working rnd, (YO, draw through 2 lps on hook) twice—long dc made.

Instructions

Square (make 63)

Center:
With variegated, ch 21.

Rnd 1 (right side):
Sc in 2nd ch from hook, and in next 19 chs; working along opposite side in unused lps of beg ch, sc in next 20 lps—40 sc.

Note: Rnds 2 through 12 are worked in continuous rnds. Do not join; mark beg of rnd.

Rnd 2:
Sc in each sc.

Rnds 3 through 12:
Rep Rnd 2. Finish off, leaving an 8" length for sewing. Weave in beg end.

Fold edges of Rnd 12 together toward center to form a square. (End of rnd will be slightly off center.) Thread end in tapestry needle and sew seam with overcast st (see Stitch Guide on page 4) through BLs only of sc.

Center Border:
Hold center with Rnd 1 facing you, seam to back side and one end of beg ch at top; with off white make lp on hook and join with an sc through both thicknesses of center in end of beg ch (between sts of Rnd 1).

Rnd 1:
2 sc in same sp—beg corner made; † ch 1, working evenly spaced along next side through both thicknesses, (sc, ch 1) 7 times; 3 sc in next corner—corner made †; rep from † to † twice more; ch 1, working evenly spaced along next side, (sc, ch 1) 7 times; join in joining sc.

Note: When changing colors at the end of a rnd, work last st until 2 lps rem on hook, draw new color through.

Rnd 2:
Sl st in next sc, ch 1, 3 sc in same sc—corner made; * † 2 sc in each of next 8 ch-1 sps †; 3 sc in 2nd sc of next corner—corner made; rep from * twice more, then rep from † to † once; join in BL of first sc, changing to coral; do not cut off white.

Rnd 3:
Ch 1, sc in same lp as joining; 3 sc through both lps of next sc; * sc in BLs of next 18 sc, 3 sc through both lps of next sc; rep from * twice more; sc in BLs of next 17 sc; join in BL of first sc, changing to off white; do not cut coral.

Rnd 4:
Ch 1, sc in same lp as joining; * † long dc (see Pattern Stitch) in 2nd sc of corner on 3rd rnd below; on working rnd, sk next sc (behind long dc), 3 sc in BL of next sc—corner made; long dc in same sc as last long dc; working in BLs only of working rnd and in unused lps of 2nd rnd below, on working rnd, sk next sc (behind long dc), sc in next sc; on 2nd rnd below, sk next lp, dc in next lp; †† on working rnd, sk next sc (behind long dc), sc in next 2 sc; on 2nd rnd below, sk next 2 lps, dc in next lp ††; rep from †† to †† 4 times more; on working rnd, sk next sc (behind dc) †; sc in next sc; rep from * twice more, then rep from † to † once; join in BL of first sc, changing to coral. Cut off white.

continued

Rnd 5:

Ch 1, sc in same lp and in BLs of next 2 sc; * † 3 long dc in 2nd sc of corner sc on 4th rnd below (where long dc of prev rnd made); on working rnd, sk next sc (behind 3 long dc) †; working in BLs only, sc in next 22 sts; rep from * twice more, then rep from † to † once; working in BLs only, sc in next 19 sc; join in first sc.

Finish off and weave in all ends.

Assembly

Join squares in 9 rows of 7 squares each. To join squares, hold 2 squares with right sides together and carefully match sts on both squares. With tapestry needle and coral, sew with overcast st (see Stitch Guide on page 4) through BLs across one side, beginning and ending in 2nd long dc of each corner. Join squares in rows; then sew rows together in same manner, being sure that all four-corner junctions are firmly joined.

Border

Hold afghan with right side facing you and one short edge at top; with coral, make lp on hook and join with an sc in 2nd long dc in upper right-hand corner; 2 sc in same sc; † sc in next 24 sts, hdc in next corner long dc (where joined), dc in joining, hdc in corner long dc on next square (where joined) †; rep from † to † 5 times more; sc in next 24 sts, 3 sc in next corner long dc—corner made; working along next side, rep from † to † 8 times; sc in next 24 sts, 3 sc in next corner long dc—corner made; working along next side, rep from † to † 6 times; sc in next 24 sts, 3 sc in next corner long dc—corner made; working along next side, rep from † to † 8 times; sc in next 24 sts; join in joining sc.

Finish off and weave in all ends.

Woven Marvel

Size:
About 42" x 57"

Materials:
Worsted weight yarn, 22 oz (1540 yds, 660 g)
off white; 7 oz (490 yds, 210 g) each of yellow,
orange, purple, magenta, teal, and rose
Size I (5.5mm) crochet hook, or size required
for gauge
Size 16 tapestry needle
Note: Photogaphed model made with Spinrite®
Berella® So Soft® Natural #9864; Sunshine
#9865; Watermelon #9867; Lilac #9850;
Magenta #9868; Aquamarine #9878;
and Strawberry #9870.

Gauge:
7 dc = 2"
one dc row = ³/₄"

Instructions

Square (make 63)

Center:
Note: Make 21 of yellow and orange (Square A), 22
of purple and magenta (Square B), and 20 of teal
and rose (Square C).

With any color, ch 22.

* Dc in 4th ch from hook (beg 3 skipped chs count as
a dc) and in each rem ch—strip made; ch 22; rep
from * 3 times more; dc in 4th ch from hook and in
each rem ch—five 20-dc strips.

Finish off and weave in all ends.

Weaving Centers:
Note: After weaving one center, you may wish to
continue with border before weaving second center.

Hold two co-ordinating centers with joined edge
of one at top and joined edge of other to right
(see photo). Weave strips. Repeat with
remaining centers.

Square Border:
Join off white through both thicknesses of joined
edges in upper right-hand corner (see photo).

Rnd 1 (right side):
Ch 3 (counts as a dc), 2 dc in same sp—beg corner
made; working across top joined edge only in sps
formed by edge dc, 3 dc in each of next 5 sps; working through both thicknesses at same time, 3 dc in
first ch of beg 3 skipped chs of top color and first
unused lp of bottom color—corner made; working
across next side in ends of strips only, 3 dc in each
strip; working through both thicknesses at same
time, 3 dc in 3rd ch of beg 3 skipped chs of top color
and first ch of beg 3 skipped chs of bottom color—
corner made; working across next side in ends of
strips only, 3 dc in each strip; working through
both thicknesses at same time, 3 dc in last dc of top
color and first dc of bottom color—corner made;
working across next side in joined edge only in sps
formed by edge dc, 3 dc in each sp; join in 3rd ch of
beg ch-3.

continued

Rnd 2:

Ch 1, sc in same ch as joining; 3 sc in next dc—corner made; * sc in next 17 dc, 3 sc in next dc—corner made; rep from * twice more; sc in next 16 dc; join in first sc.

Finish off and weave in all ends.

Assembly

Referring to Diagram A for placement, join squares in 9 rows of 7 squares each. To join, hold 2 blocks with right sides together carefully matching stitches. With tapestry needle and matching yarn, sew with overcast stitch (see Stitch Guide on page 4) through BLs only along one edge, beginning and ending in 2nd sc of each corner. Join squares in rows, then sew rows together in same manner, being sure that all four-corner junctions are firmly joined.

Border

Note: On following rnd, each seam is counted as a stitch.

Hold afghan with one short end at top, join off white in 2nd sc of upper right-hand corner; ch 4 (counts as a dc and a ch-1 sp), in same sp work (dc, ch 1) 3 times; dc in same sp—beg shell corner made; † sk next 3 sts, sl st in next st, sk next 2 sts, in next st work (dc, ch 1) 4 times; dc in same st—shell made; †† sk next 2 sts, sl st in next st, sk next 2 sts, in next st work (dc, ch 1) 4 times; dc in same st—shell made ††; rep from †† to †† 20 times more; sk next 2 sts, sl st in next st, sk next 3 sts, in next st work (dc, ch 1) 4 times; dc in same st—shell corner made †; rep from †† to †† 28 times; sk next 2 sts, sl st in next st, sk next 2 sts, in next st work (dc, ch 1) 4 times; dc in same st—shell corner made; rep from † to † once; rep from †† to †† 29 times; sk next 2 sts, sl st in next st, sk next 2 sts; join in 3rd ch of beg ch-4.

Finish off and weave in all ends.

Diagram A

B	A	C	B	C	A	B
A	C	B	A	B	C	A
C	B	A	C	A	B	C
B	A	C	B	C	A	B
A	C	B	A	B	C	A
B	A	C	B	C	A	B
C	B	A	C	A	B	C
A	C	B	A	B	C	A
B	A	C	B	C	A	B

Winding Rosebuds

Size:
About 45" x 58"

Materials:
Worsted weight yarn, 48 oz **(3360 yds, 1440 g)**
  off white; 6 oz **(420 yds, 180 g)** green; 3 oz
  (210 yds, 90 g) red
Size I **(5.5mm)** crochet hook, or size required
  for gauge
Note: Photographed model made with Caron
  Wintuk® Off White #3002; Fir #3010;
  and Strawberry #3057.

Gauge:
4 dc = 1"
4 dc rows = 3"

Pattern Stitches

Cluster (CL):
YO, insert hook in FL of sc just worked, YO, draw
through 2 lps on hook, YO, insert hook in next st
indicated on 2nd rnd below, YO, draw through
2 lps on hook, YO, on working rnd, sk st behind st
worked on 2nd rnd below, insert hook in FL of
next sc, YO, draw through 2 lps on hook; with
color indicated, YO and draw through all 4 lps on
hook—CL made.

Long Single Crochet Cluster (long sc CL):
YO, insert hook in FL of next sc on 2nd rnd below,
draw up lp to height of working rnd, **(**YO, insert
hook in same lp and draw up lp to height of working rnd**)** twice; with color indicated, YO and draw
through all 7 lps on hook—long sc CL made.
Note: Sk st behind long sc CL on working rnd.

Long Double Crochet (long dc):
YO, insert hook in sp indicated, draw up lp to
height of working rnd, **(**YO, draw through 2 lps on
hook**)** twice—long dc made. **Note:** Sk st behind
long dc on working rnd.

V-Stitch Cluster (V-st CL):
YO, insert hook in FL of st indicated on 2nd rnd
below, YO, draw through 2 lps on hook, sk next
long sc CL, YO, insert hook in FL of next sc on
2nd rnd below, YO, draw through 2 lps on hook;
with color indicated, YO and draw through all
3 lps on hook—V-st CL made.

Long Single Crochet (long sc):
Insert hook in st indicated, YO and draw up lp to
height of working rnd, YO and draw through 2 lps
on hook—long sc made.

Instructions

Panel (make 8)

Center Braid
With off white, ch 635, mark 316th ch from beg.

In 5th ch from hook work **(**dc, ch 1**)** 3 times (beg 4
skipped chs count as a dc and a ch-1 sp); dc in same
ch—beg 5-dc group made; dc in next 2 chs; keeping
last lp of each dc on hook, **(**sk next ch, dc in next ch**)**
5 times; YO and draw through all 6 lps on hook—
cluster made; dc in next 2 chs; † in next ch work **(**dc,
ch 1**)** 4 times; dc in same ch—5-dc group made; dc
in next 2 chs; keeping last lp of each dc on hook **(**sk
next ch, dc in next ch**)** 5 times; YO and draw through
all 6 lps on hook—cluster made; dc in next 2 chs †;
rep from † to † 19 times more; in marked ch work
(dc, ch 1**)** 9 times; dc in same ch—10-dc group
made; dc in next 2 chs; keeping last lp of each dc on
hook **(**sk next ch, dc in next ch**)** 5 times; YO and
draw through all 6 lps on hook—cluster made; dc in
next 2 chs; rep from † to † 20 times; in next ch work
(dc, ch 1**)** 5 times—ending 5-dc group made; draw
up long lp on hook, remove hook, do not cut yarn.

continued

Hold center braid with 10-dc group at top; weave sides over and under each other (see photo); at opposite end, re-insert hook in long lp and join in 3rd ch of beg 4 skipped chs, forming a second 10-dc group. Weave beg yarn end through base of ending 5-dc group to hold 10-dc group together.

Center Border:
Rnd 1:
Ch 1, 2 sc in same ch; working in BLs only of dc and chs, 2 sc in each of next 4 sts; ch 4, working along next side, † sc in unused lp at base of 3rd dc of next cluster, ch 4, sc in BL of 3rd dc of next 5-dc group, ch 4 †; rep from † to † 19 times more; †† sc in unused lp at base of 3rd dc of next cluster, ch 4, working around next end, 2 sc in BL of 3rd dc of next 10-dc group ††; working in BLs only of chs and dc, 2 sc in each of next 10 sts; ch 4; rep from † to † 20 times; rep from †† to †† once; working in BLs only of chs and dc, 2 sc in each of next 6 sts; join in BL of first sc.

Rnd 2:
Ch 1, sc in same lp; working in BLs only, sc in next 9 sc, 4 sc in next ch-4 sp; † sc in next sc, 4 sc in next ch-4 sp †; rep from † to † 40 times more; sc in next 22 sc, 4 sc in next ch-4 sp; rep from † to † 41 times; sc in next 12 sc; join in BL of first sc until needed.

Note: When changing colors, work last st until 2 lps rem on hook, draw new color through. Carry color not in use, working over carried strand until needed.

Rnd 3:
Ch 1, sc in same lp; working in BLs only, sc in next sc, (2 sc in next sc, sc in next sc) twice; sc in next 3 sc, changing to green in last sc; † CL (see Pattern Stitches on page 17) over FL of sc just worked, FL of next ch on center braid and FL of next sc on working rnd, changing to off white; sc in BL of sc just worked and in next 8 sc, changing to green in last sc; †† CL over FL of sc just worked, FL of next dc on center braid and FL of next sc on working rnd, changing to off white; sc in BL of sc just worked and in next 8 sc, changing to green in last sc ††; rep from †† to †† 19 times more; CL over FL of sc just worked, FL of next ch on center braid and FL of next sc on working rnd, changing to off white; sc in BL of sc just worked and in next 4 sc, (2 sc in next sc, sc in next sc) twice; sc in next sc changing to green †; CL over FL of sc just worked, FL of next ch on center braid and FL of next sc on working rnd, changing to off white; working in BLs only, sc in sc just worked and in next sc, (2 sc in next sc, sc in next sc) twice; sc in next 3 sc, changing to green in last sc; rep from † to † once; CL over FL of sc just worked, FL of next ch on center braid and FL of first sc, changing to off white; join in BL of first sc. Finish off green.

Rnd 4:

Ch 1, sc in same lp, working in BLs only, sc in next 4 sc, changing to red in last sc; long sc CL (see Pattern Stitches on page 17) in FL of next sc on 2nd rnd below, changing to off white; on working rnd, sc in BLs of next 10 sc, changing to red in last sc; † long sc CL in FL of next sc on 2nd rnd below, changing to off white; on working rnd, sc in BLs of next 9 sc, changing to red in last sc †; rep from † to † 19 times more; †† long sc CL in FL of next sc on 2nd rnd below, changing to off white; on working rnd, sc in BLs of next 11 sc, changing to red in last sc ††; rep from †† to †† once more; long sc CL in FL of next sc on 2nd rnd below, changing to off white; on working rnd, sc in BLs of next 10 sc, changing to red in last sc; rep from † to † 20 times; rep from †† to †† once; long sc CL in FL of next sc on 2nd rnd below, changing to off white; on working rnd, sc in BLs of next 6 sc; join in BL of first sc. Finish off red.

Rnd 5:

Ch 1, sc in same lp as joining; † long dc (see Pattern Stitches on page 17) in FL of next sc on 2nd rnd below; on working rnd, sc in BL of next sc †; rep from † to † once, changing to green in last sc; V-st CL (see Pattern Stitches on page 17) over FL of sc on 2nd rnd below sc just worked, next long sc CL, and FL of next sc on 2nd rnd below, changing to off white; on working rnd, sc in BL of sc behind sc just worked; rep from † to † 4 times; sc in BL of next sc, changing to green; †† V-st CL over FL of sc on 2nd rnd below sc just worked, next long sc CL, and FL of next sc on 2nd rnd below, changing to off white; on working rnd, sc in BL of sc behind sc just worked and in next sc; rep from † to † 3 times; sc in BL of next sc, changing to green ††; rep from †† to †† 19 times more; V-st CL over FL of sc on 2nd rnd below sc just worked, next long sc CL, and FL of next sc on 2nd rnd below, changing to off white; on working rnd, sc in BL of sc behind sc just worked and in next sc; rep from † to † 4 times; sc in BL of next sc, changing to green; V-st CL over FL of sc on 2nd rnd below sc just worked, next long sc CL, and FL of next sc on 2nd rnd below, changing to off white; on working rnd, sc in BL of sc behind sc just worked; rep from † to † 5 times, changing to green in last sc; V-st CL over FL of sc on 2nd rnd below sc just worked, next long sc CL, and FL of next sc on 2nd rnd below, changing to off white; on working rnd, sc in BL of sc behind sc just worked; rep from † to † 4 times; sc in BL of next sc, changing to green; rep from †† to †† 20 times; V-st CL over FL of sc on 2nd rnd below sc just worked, next long sc CL, and FL of next sc on 2nd rnd below, changing to off white; on working rnd, sc in BL of sc behind sc just worked and in next sc; rep from † to † 4 times; sc in BL of next sc, changing to green; V-st CL over FL of sc on 2nd rnd below sc just worked, next long sc CL, and FL of next sc on 2nd rnd below, changing to off white; on working rnd, sc in BL of sc behind sc just worked; rep from † to † twice; long dc in FL of next sc on 2nd rnd below; join in BL of first sc. Finish off green.

Rnd 6:

Sl st in BL of next dc, ch 1, sc in same lp; long dc in FL of next sc on 2nd rnd below; on working rnd, sc in BL of next 2 sts, working over V-st CL, long sc (see Pattern Stitches on page 17) in next long sc CL on 2nd rnd below; sc in BLs of next 2 sts; † long dc in FL of next sc on 2nd rnd below; on working rnd, sc in BL of next st †; rep from † to † 3 times more; †† long sc in next long sc CL on 2nd rnd below; on working rnd, sc in BL of next sc; rep from † to † 4 times ††; rep from †† to †† 19 times more; long sc in next long sc CL on 2nd rnd below; on working rnd, sc in BL of next sc; rep from † to † 5 times; long sc in next long sc CL on 2nd rnd below; on working rnd, sc in BL of next 2 sts; rep from † to † 4 times; sc in BL of next sc, long sc in next long sc CL on 2nd rnd below; on working rnd, sc in BL of next 2 sts; rep from † to † 4 times; rep from †† to †† 20 times; long sc in next long sc CL on 2nd rnd below; on working rnd, sc in BL of next sc; rep from † to † 5 times; long sc in next long sc CL on 2nd rnd below; on working rnd, sc in BL of next 2 sts; rep from † to † twice; long dc in FL of joining sc on 2nd rnd below; join in first sc.

Finish off and weave in all ends.

continued

Winding Rosebuds

Assembly
Hold two panels with right sides together; beginning
and ending with sc above first CL along side and
working through BLs only, sew together using overcast st (see Stitch Guide on page 4). Repeat with
remaining panels.

Border
Hold afghan with one short end at top, with off
white, make lp on hook and join with an sc through
both lps of last sc of first panel in upper right-hand
corner (where joined to second panel); working
around outer edge through both lps, sc in first long
dc of second panel (first st after joining to first
panel); * † ch 2, sk next st, sc in next st †; rep from
† to † 11 times more; sc in first long dc of next panel
(first st after joining); rep from * 5 times more; rep
from † to † around outer edge of 8th panel to first
seam on opposite short end; ** sc in first long dc of
next panel; rep from † to † 12 times; rep from ** 5
times more; sc in first long dc of next panel; rep
from † to † to joining sc; join in joining sc.

Finish off and weave in all ends.